TWO CHAPTERS

IN THE

LAW OF TORTS.

I.—*THE REASONABLE MAN.*

II.—*THE UNKNOWN WORKMAN.*

BY

FRANCIS TAYLOR PIGGOTT,

OF THE MIDDLE TEMPLE, BARRISTER-AT-LAW; PROCUREUR AND ADVOCATE-
GENERAL, MAURITIUS; LATE LEGAL ADVISER
TO THE JAPANESE CABINET.

LONDON:

WILLIAM CLOWES AND SONS, LIMITED,

Law Publishers and Booksellers,

27, FLEET STREET.

1898.

Price One Shilling and Sixpence.

TWO CHAPTERS

IN THE

LAW OF TORTS.

TWO CHAPTERS IN THE
LAW OF TORTS.

———◦◦◦———

I.

THE REASONABLE MAN.

I HAVE accepted, with the greatest possible pleasure, the invitation of your President to address you to-day; but I will freely confess that that pleasure has not been wholly unalloyed, for, giving me the whole range of Law, he desired me to choose my own subject. Thereupon a whole army of subjects presented themselves for my consideration; there came flitting by me ghosts of ideas which once had half persuaded me to discuss them, but which had died of inanition when my good intentions had sunk into the pavement of the nether world. I was tempted to talk to you of the history and tradition of our law, and to excite your admiration for a system which compels us to seek its doctrines in books written in a quite forgotten language, and in characters which have long since passed into obscurity and which only those may read who loiter by the way. Or to expatiate to you on the subtle beauties of a law whose perfect whole is divided into two parts, that which is known and has already been expounded, and that which is only unknown because the occasion for its exposition has not yet arisen. The charm and perfection of the matter is that this unknown part always remains the greater; fifteen years' study finds me not much further from the threshold than you who have but just opened our text-books. Yet this unknown law is a written law, as you well know, the roll of it being variously and curiously described as " The Clouds," or " The Judicial Bosom." I was tempted, too, to discuss the merits of an unwritten law as compared with those of a Code: but though I can scarcely avoid touching on the question, I am in public duty bound to say nothing that should in any way tend to make you dissatisfied with the great projects of your Government in the matter of Codes, even if I thought, which assuredly I do not, that there existed any better way of dealing with so momentous a national problem. Again, I was tempted to unravel for you some of those written mysteries which are to be found in what is facetiously termed " The Statute Book," but which after much patient revision and excision of dead parts is hardly to be contained in five-and-twenty very ponderous and portly volumes: but I could do nothing which should in the slightest degree incite the *principes* and *sapientes* of this Eastern Kingdom to follow the example of the British legislator who makes of the path of duty a labyrinth wherein not even the wariest can walk with safety. I trust that the Japanese lawyers will never have this means furnished to them for growing rich.

But, because I am an English lawyer who is not a little proud of his law, and because you are Japanese who are eager to study it, I felt that I must talk to you somewhat more specifically of the great Common Law of England. For in spite of the cohort of Continental lawyers who, most harmoniously I feel sure, have assisted your own lawyers in the perfection and elaboration of your new Codes, I believe that the study of English law, in the peculiar method of its training, will work for much good to you who have willingly subjected yourselves to it ; and in the results of that method, when you have attained the goals of your ambition, will work for infinite benefit to the community, who will derive assistance and receive judgment at your hands. I mean in this to pay something more than a passing compliment to your school. I believe, that when that good time comes, and your Sovereign looks for " such as know the law and mean duly to observe it " to represent him in his courts, and to do the right on his behalf between his people, between those who owe him full allegiance and those who owe him temporary allegiance, he will choose many of them from among those who studied English law in this school and have received their diplomas from its distinguished professors. For the peculiar methods of thought, which the duty of ascertaining the law applicable to any given set of circumstances under an unwritten law imposes, are those which go far to make up the qualifications of a good judge. Every case that presents itself for opinion comes as a problem in favour of whose solution either way there are instances without end to be cited. An acute advocate could argue for either side, citing case upon case in favour of his various contentions; but the advice which he has to give in his chambers upon the case, and the judgment which the judge has to pronounce upon it from the bench, demand equally a calm and dispassionate holding of the balance between the conflict of opposing analogies. And therefore it is that the judicial habit of mind has to be assumed by English lawyers with the very first brief with which it is their good fortune to be entrusted.

The soul of English law finds expression in one word, Precedent: and I believe that the rule of law is stronger when it is based on a law of precedent than it is when it depends on a law of rules. Precedent must always be weak when the Court seeks the law in the rule and not in the example. The form in which a case presents itself to the mind of the judge is: Does the case come within a given rule of law? He is disinclined, unless he is obliged, to look at other cases to which other judges have applied the rule. With us the question is: Does the case come within such and such an interpretation of a given rule? The judge is bound to follow in the steps of those of equal or higher degree who have had the same question before them. And if, as I was half persuaded to, I had made my address to you one "in praise of English law," I should have set this rule of precedent in the foremost place. For it is in this respect, I believe I am not wrong in saying, that the administration of English law differs so considerably from that of the law of other European nations.

Again I come back to that interesting question, What influence can the study of English law have on Japanese law? I have answered it once: it will train good judges. I now give a second answer: it may help to make the rule of precedent the guiding principle for the interpretation of the Codes.

I propose, however, to discuss with you to-day the spirit of the English Common Law.

And to this end I shall talk to you about a most interesting person who is the creation of that law and who probably is not altogether unfamiliar to you: he is called the reasonable man. His character, however, is not yet fully developed: and the reason for this will be apparent from what I have already said: but the Courts are busy the year through, the long summer days excepted, in perfecting it. Not a day passes but some fresh quality is added to, or some fresh example is given of his already delightful character. Who and what is he? He is a man only of average intellect and intelligence, and not transcendently wise. He is very human: his wisdom is only of the common worldly sort; he cannot foresee the unexpected; though he learns from past experience, he is not one of whom we say contemptuously he is wise after the event; acting circumspectly himself, he is not extreme with his neighbours, requiring them to be more than careful; he begs them only to act circumspectly too; he is most particular not to do harm to his fellows deliberately; and when he does injure them we cannot blame him, for we know that it must have been from sheer necessity, or that it was unintentional and that things could scarcely have happened otherwise. Indeed, he will often avoid causing people trouble which after all every one would have said had served them right. Do you not recognize him in this sketch? Let me fill in some details from some very familiar examples of his behaviour in everyday life. He sees a donkey tied up in the middle of the Ginza, and tied up too by some very careless person; he does not drive over it, you may be sure; he will avoid it if he possibly can, and so spare the donkey's feelings, its master's purse, and his own carriage. When he orders a workman to come to his house to repair the paper of the *shoji*, he will be careful not only to tell his boy to close the trap-door in the passage, but he will see to it himself lest the workman should be unfortunate enough to trip over it. If he is stopping at the Fujiya at Miyanoshita, he will not ask a pretty *nesan* to fetch the gun he has left upstairs, unless he is quite sure that it is not loaded : does he not know that *nesan* are inquisitive little maidens? and it would be cruel, unwise, unreasonable, to put so frail a daughter of Eve (Isanami is, I think, our first mother's Japanese name) in so imminent and great a danger. He digs a well close to the highway. He knows that many people come and go along it by night and day, and some less warily than others, according to their nature; and though the well is in his own plot of land, he is careful to fence it round lest the unwary stumble and fall into it. And if he speaks of others concerning their credit he will speak discreetly, saying only such things as he knows or believes to be true, lest the person who has questioned him should act to his own or to that other's detriment. But sometimes in this matter of spreading evil report, a sense of duty will compel him to speak, though he is not sure that the report is true; yet in such cases he will speak without malice, and only to such persons as have a direct interest in knowing the report whether it be true or false. And so, less particularly, he keeps his savage dog securely chained up, lest it rush out and bite the passers-by; his vicious horse is kept within his paddock, lest it stray upon the highway and kick the neighbour's children at their play; his bridges that span public roads are well looked after, lest the mortar should decay with time, and the bricks, being shaken, fall on inoffensive heads; his wire fences are always in good repair, lest his neighbours' cattle eat the rusty strands and die, or get through and, after their nature, fight his own beasts so that both are injured. These and such-like things you know the reasonable man will assuredly do. But, as I have said, he is only a reasonable man, not a very reasonable man; and therefore there are many things which you cannot expect him to do. Thus, if he digs a well in his garden, but at some distance from the highway, he will warn those who come upon his land legitimately and whom he may expect to come there; but he will not necessarily fence it, for those who do not come there by his leave or on his business are trespassers, and with such he has no concern. He is not careful of those who know of dangers and deliberately incur the risks. He does not fence in the roof of his house when he tells a workman to mend the tiles, or gives an artist leave to sit there to take a bird's-eye view of the great city below.

I think these few examples of the good he does, and the evils we cannot blame him for, will suffice to remind you of the position which this interesting personage fills in English law. His character is the model to which on all occasions we have to conform in our everyday life and dealings with our neighbours. I say on all occasions deliberately, although, as you well know, in many parts of the Common Law the duties laid down are of a character more precise than that of conforming to what perhaps is after all only an imperfectly defined ideal. That part of the law which deals with contracts lends itself more readily to the formation of precise rules; in commercial affairs the circumstances of one case are often identical with those of another. What happens to-day when A contracts with B will happen to-morrow when B contracts with C, the next day when C contracts with D, and so on through the year and through the alphabet. So in the Law of Torts, concerning the many things which, alas for poor humanity, are happening every day (in Europe, at least), the assaults and batteries, the frauds, the libels, the conversions, and the trespasses, it has been possible to lay down and elaborate many precise rules, which are practically the legal translation of the sixth, seventh, eighth, and ninth paragraphs of the old Jewish Law; and when you study the law applicable to these special subjects, you are studying the thousand and one illustrations of the way in which these simple duties have been broken by the weaker brethren. You learn, for example, that a threat, even when there is no actual violence, may be an assault; that the least touching of another in anger is a battery; that to tell a tradesman he may trust your friend whom you know to be insolvent is fraudulent; that to say of a barrister, " He is no lawyer," is to slander him; that to withhold another's property amounts to a conversion; and that to walk in another man's garden is a trespass. But though these elementary rules of the Law of Torts, and the equally elementary rules of the Law of Contract, are simple, well-known, and precise, they are none the less the rules by which the reasonable man will regulate his behaviour. They are not arbitrary, nor are they difficult either to understand or conform to. In judging of men who have violated them, it is not necessary to make a direct appeal to our ideal, simply because long experience has taught us that they are of the very essence of his daily regard for his neighbours. But when you get away from these simple rules and begin, in either of the two great branches of the Common Law, to inquire more deeply into any of these special matters, to examine the limits and exceptions to the fundamental rules, you come at once to the appeal to the ideal, you find at once the question of right and wrong determined upon by direct reference to the standard of the reasonable man. Take for example so simple a case in the Law of Contracts as the interpretation of the rule you doubtless are very familiar with, that " Time is not of the

essence of the Contract :" this means not only that goo
must be paid for if they are delivered within reasonab
time whether so soon as they are wanted or not ; be
also that they need not be taken unless they are
delivered : " reasonable time " meaning, of course, th
time which our friend the reasonable man, if he had th
order, would have taken to deliver the goods. And
it is in the specific branches of the Law of Torts. Su
a threat as " If you are not quiet I will blow your brai
out," will be an assault or not according as the fear
bodily harm which the words engender is or is n
reasonable. The law only allows a person assaulted
lay gentle hands on his assailant ; and if he is unreaso
able in his defence he is himself guilty of an assault an
battery. A statement made in answer to a question, as
a man's credit, for instance, though untrue, is not fraud
lent if the speaker had reasonable grounds for believin
it to be true. The whole of that part of the Law
Libel which deals with privilege, and which exemp
from liability those who speak what is false concernin
others, makes the privilege depend on whether in spea
ing they have behaved reasonably or not. A conve
sion is justified if there were reasonable grounds f
believing that the goods belonged to a third perso
A trespass even is justified by necessity, which mea
nothing else than a reasonable necessity ; as where
certain river overflowed and had rendered the towpath
impassable, the towers were held justified in going
to the adjoining field, yet only on that part of it ne
the river.

But these well-known and specific branches of the Law of Torts do not contain the expression of the whole duty of man to his neighbours. There is, as you well know, a very large portion of that law which, under the head of Negligence, deals with all those thousand and one complex incidents of daily life which give rise to what are called accidents, but as to which it is impossible to lay down any precise definitions of duty. The law does not say, for example, and indeed it could not say, you may not drive a carriage through the street, in the same way that it says you may not strike another; it does not say you may not keep a restive horse in your field, in the same way that it says you may not walk in another man's garden. But what it does say is, if you do drive a carriage through the street, you must drive it carefully—that is, without negligence; if you do keep a restive horse in your field, you must take proper precautions to keep him from straying out of it. A number of similar examples will occur to all of you who have learnt the elements merely of the law of negligence. In the two that I have given, and in the many which you will remember, there occur certain expressions which so far as ordinary language goes are perfectly intelligible, but which, when we come to look more deeply into the matter, we find are wanting in the precision which ought to characterize legal language, more especially when it is dealing with matters so important as right and duty. These expressions are : carelessly, improperly, recklessly, negligently, and so on. But if the breach of duty be thus

B

expressed, the duty itself must also be capable of expression in corresponding terms, thus: on such and such occasions to act with care, properly, heedfully, or without negligence. But what does acting properly mean unless there is somewhere to be found a standard of propriety? or what does acting negligently mean unless we know of some standard enabling us to draw a line on the one side of which will lie acts to be deemed wrongful as being done with negligence, and on the other side acts to be deemed not wrongful as being done without negligence? It is this standard which the English law supplies in the person of the reasonable man; and its broad canon of behaviour is, on all occasions, at all times and in all seasons, to conform to this standard.

It is of the utmost importance that you should fully appreciate the way this standard is arrived at, and I beg your attention most particularly to this matter, as it is a little confusing, and many writers have not succeeded in making the principle perfectly plain. A very learned American author puts this case: "Suppose a blacksmith were to find a watch by the roadside, and discovering it to be full of dirt and gathering rust, should attempt to clean it and put it in order, and in doing so, though exercising the greatest care, should injure the watch; if we have to answer the question, did he act as a prudent man in his situation might have done? the answer could not but be in the affirmative, for a watchmaker would have done the same thing." This does seem at first sight to be the result of the reference to an ideal. But in truth the answer would be in the negative. In the inquiries did this person act reasonably? or, did he act as a reasonable man would have done under the same circumstances? the point, as I understand the law, at which we wish to arrive is, assuming him to be a reasonable man, did he act reasonably or unreasonably on this occasion? To determine whether a blacksmith acted reasonably or not under certain circumstances, we do not compare his conduct with that of reasonable men in the abstract, nor with that of reasonable specialists in the concrete; but simply with reasonable blacksmiths. In inquiring whether that blacksmith did act reasonably or not, we are compelled, it is true, to set up an ideal; but it is an ideal blacksmith, and nothing else. And so, to bring this question down to matters of more frequent occurrence, such as driving in thoroughfares, it seems clear that what would be reasonable for one might be unreasonable for another. For example, what would be reasonable for a man to do in an emergency who was skilled in the management of horses, would very probably be unreasonable for one unskilled to attempt. The ideals would be, in the first case, the conduct of the reasonable skilled man; in the second, the conduct of the reasonable unskilled man. And generally, in order to determine whether what a man has done is reasonable or not, we must put in his place and under precisely the same conditions a reasonable man, and endeavour to ascertain what he would have done under the circumstances. If what the man in fact did does not conform to this standard, then the law says that he has acted unreasonably, and is guilty of negligence.

The method by which the standard is arrived at is an interesting one; both judge and jury have a share in determining it. The cases are easily divisible into three classes. In the first we find the judge declaring that the case speaks for itself, that on the face of it the duty was clear, and therefore that no special evidence of negligence is necessary. As, where two trains come into collision, it is evident that some one has blundered, and it is for the defendant to show the contrary if he can. In the second class of cases we find the judge declaring that on the facts before the Court there is no evidence of a breach of duty: these are cases which in common language we should call accidents. A man is driving slowly down the street on a dark night, another is crossing with all due care, but he slips and falls under the horses' feet. There is no negligence here, and an action would inevitably end in a nonsuit. The third class of cases lies midway between the other two: and as to these I cannot do more now than state the rule by which they are governed, leaving it to you to trace its application in your private studies. It is the duty of the judge to say whether any facts have been established by evidence from which negligence *may* be reasonably inferred: the jury has then to say whether, from those facts, negligence *ought* to be inferred. So, then, you have these three classes of cases—those in which negligence *must* be found; those in which it *cannot* be found; and those in which it *may* be found: or, those in which it is clear that a reasonable man would not have acted as the defendant did; those in which it is equally clear that a reasonable man would have acted as the defendant did; and those in which it is doubtful as to how a reasonable man would have acted, and the assistance of a jury (presumed themselves to be reasonable men) has to be invoked to determine the matter. I have given you in this sketch the merest outline of the law concerning reasonable men, but the outline would be incomplete if I did not trespass still further on your patience and show you how the same idea runs through that branch of the law which you know as " Contributory Negligence." Many an accident is brought about through the carelessness of the injured person himself. If a man, for example, runs recklessly across a street in which there are many carriages, and gets knocked down by one of them, whose fault is it but his own? He will have to pay the doctor's bill himself. But this does not dispose of the whole matter. The law, in requiring all men to conform to the standard of reason, requires it on all occasions, even when they have to deal with foolish and unreasonable people. A reasonable man, if it is possible, will avoid injuring even an unreasonable man. And therefore, in the case I have supposed of a man running across a crowded thorough-fare, it is the duty of a driver, even though he is not driving recklessly, to pull out of the way if he can. If he could have avoided running over the man, and did not, the blame and the doctor's bill will rest with him.

Once again I must enunciate the rule and leave the application of it to you : first, a plaintiff cannot recover if with ordinary care he could have avoided the consequences of the defendant's negligence ; secondly, a plaintiff can recover if the defendant with ordinary care could have avoided the consequences of the plaintiff's negligence.

Apply these rules for yourselves to the case of the donkey tied up in the middle of the Ginza, and you will find that under some circumstances, if the axle of the carriage is broken in driving over the animal, the donkey-man will have to pay : and under other circumstances, if the donkey's leg is broken, the driver of the carriage will have to pay. And if I held the brief for a poor little *nesan* who has been injured by the loaded gun she has been sent to fetch, and Mr. Masujima for the defendant should urge that it was her own fault, that her inquisitiveness was to blame and not his client, I should answer him thus : it is the height of unreason first, to leave loaded guns about at all ; and secondly, to send a not too reasonable, though delightful, attendant to fetch such a thing ; thirdly, if he would do these things, not to foresee that what happened was almost inevitable, unless the little cherub who looks after the lives of *nesan* had providentially diverted the bullet in its course. I can see in your faces that his client would receive short shrift from you, were you his judges, and that O Kiku-san would get her verdict with substantial damages : and you may find good cause for your judgment if you learn with diligence those chapters in the Book of our Law, which are entitled "Contributory Negligence" and "Remoteness of Damage." This, then, is the substance of the whole matter. The English law, in judging of men's behaviour whether it is right or wrong, refers it to an ideal, but not to a very lofty one. Having so much to do with the petty affairs of everyday life—with the walking and the talking, with the driving along the streets, and the keeping of dogs and monkeys—it endeavours to ascertain and appreciate the springs which influence the smallest of human actions ; it endeavours to understand the weaker as well as the stronger side of human nature, and with the materials thus gathered, makes of its ideal quite a simple ordinary mortal; having to judge of things which happen in the byways as well as in the highways of existence, it endows him with the characters of those who saunter along village lanes, as well as of those whose life is spent in the busy throng of cities. It does not insist on his leading the life of a recluse, rejoicing rather to see him mix with the throng, and going where his fellows most do congregate. And having thus created an ideal it sets him to work to infuse a sweet reasonableness into the lives of men. His is a character which I think should be especially appreciated by Japanese, for, as you will have observed, in many things it much resembles theirs.

Let me, in conclusion, express a hope that those who administer your Codes and those to whom your Constitution gives authority will find you all, if not perfectly reasonable, at least not unreasonable men.

II.

THE UNKNOWN WORKMAN.

On the last occasion when I had the honour of addressing you, I spoke at some length concerning the reasonable man. To-day I propose to talk to you about the position which another prominent person in everyday life holds in English law. Him I call the Unknown Workman.

In my former lecture I endeavoured to show you that the English Common Law, unscientific, chaotic, as many of its critics contend that it is, does rest, if we tread the track through a very forest of decisions, on a substantial basis of principle. On this basis all the great edifice of our case law has been reared : to this principle all the appalling array of our rules has an ultimate reference. The English law, in establishing its great canon that all men must at all times and in all seasons conform to the standard of reason, and in leaving the standard itself to be determined by twelve men drawn promiscuously from the reasonable community, endeavours to fulfil the great function of law ; in order that the right or the wrong of any human action may be determined, to appreciate the springs of human actions in general, and above all to study the weak side of human nature as well as the strong. And so our law requires conformity to a standard which is no utopian ideal, but is based on the common course of conduct among the community to which the person belongs whose action has to be judged. A deep insight into the lives ruled can alone give satisfactory rules of living. This intimate connection between law and life it is which gives vitality to the law—a vitality evidenced not by the multitude of the occasions on which its majestic existence is made manifest by rigorous enforcement, but by the silent unconscious everyday obedience to it. A closer connection between the springs of law and the springs of life it is impossible to find, look we the whole world over, than in the great Common Law of England.

It is on the silent obedience to the spirit of the law that I dwell to-day, on its necessity in all the unobserved, the unseen actions of the work-a-day world, and on the complete dependence of the well-being of the community upon it. The consideration of this question brings into very strong relief the weakness of the law : its powerlessness to enforce obedience to its rules on a thousand occasions on which disobedience to them may work incalculable harm, may bring death or disaster to many. In cases innumerable the actual wrong-doer cannot be discovered ; he is one among the hundred who have contributed to the creation of the machine, for example, which has suddenly broken down, but it would pass the wit of man to dis- cover him and bring his negligence home. So the wrong-doer goes unpunished, and if there is no vicarious liability in another person, or if some other negligent person has not intervened to change the natural or probable current of events, the person injured has no redress.

This weakness is common both to codified and uncodified bodies of law, and the one is not more elastic than the other.

I pause for a moment to correct in anticipation an erroneous conclusion which I know that some of you will draw from some of my remarks, and to refute a statement which has recently appeared in print. You know at once to what I allude : it is inevitable that I should touch incidentally upon it; it is the attitude of English lawyers towards codification.

A learned author has said by implication—somewhat irrelevantly, it must be confessed, to the question then in hand—that English lawyers oppose codification because it would touch their pockets. From so wise a mouth never yet came so unwise an utterance. It will not be out of place, however, that you, students of English law, should fully understand the opinions of English lawyers on a subject which is of such importance to your own country.

A lawyer would forfeit his claim to sanity if he opposed codification simply. The merits of codification are not to be discussed generally, but specially with a view to the necessities of any given country. Now, with regard to codification for England, there are some who doubt whether it is practical, and there are others who doubt whether any specific good would come of it in the way of making the law clearer or reducing the amount of litigation ; for a Code, after all, is not a royal road for making people behave themselves and preventing them quarrelling. Well, as I say, some English lawyers may hold strong views on the subject of codification for England ; but that subject has no interest at all for you : it has nothing whatever to do with the question of codification for Japan. And if your admiration for English law is so great as to lead you to think that at this momentous time of your national history It would have been better to do without Codes, that you might now safely wait till a fabric of law like our Common Law has been built by your diligence and erudition, believe me you are profoundly in error. Codes in Japan were inevitable, and not regrettable. But what I said to you before, I say to you again : the virtue of what you are so intelligently learning, the efficacy of the skilful training you are receiving in English law, will reveal themselves when the good time comes, and the joy of argumentative strife waxes fast and furious round the articles of your Codes, and the big briefs roll in upon you.

Let us now go back to our subject—the unknown workman—and study some familiar illustrations of the consequences of his carelessness, and the way in which the law deals with them. You are walking in the street ; a cask rolls out upon your head from the upper window of a godown. As you are going into a shop a pile of packages set up in the doorway tumbles down upon you, or a piece of glass falls from the window of a neighbouring shop which has been broken by a ladder falling against it.   Some one evidently must have set the cask down, or piled up the packages, or left the ladder standing carelessly ; or some one must deliberately or negligently have knocked them down.   The chances are that in such case it was some careless workman who has gone home to his dinner, and it is beyond your power to find him.   Well, the law helps you to redress by making an assumption.   Neither barrels, nor cases, nor ladders fall of their own accord : there must have been negligence somewhere.   Therefore, where it is reasonable to assume that this negligence was that of the servants of the owner of the premises, the law says " the thing speaks for itself ; " it holds the master liable unless he can rebut the presumption, as by showing that an earthquake had tumbled them over.   This is the principle *res ipsa loquitur ;* and its application to the three cases just mentioned is as follows.   The owner of the godown will be liable because they are his servants only who touch the barrels stored there.   For the same reason the shopman will be liable, because none but his servants can have stacked the cases at his door.   But the owner of the adjoining premises whose windows were broken by the falling ladder will not be liable, for some one else over whom he had no control, for whose acts he is not vicariously liable, may have left it in an insecure position or kicked it over : the ladder was not necessarily used in his own business, and therefore the assumption of law cannot be applied, the facts of themselves do not warrant any definite conclusion. You have no redress unless you can find the wrong-doer. Here, then, is an instance of the unknown workman going scot-free, and no one being liable on his behalf.

Let us take another case which is dealt with on another principle. A man is walking along the highway and passes under a railway bridge. A brick falls out of the bridge and injures him. It may have been loosened by frost, but it must have been the frost of many nights, not of one, and therefore only one conclusion is possible: the railway company were bound to keep their bridges in repair; the bridge was out of repair and caused damage; therefore they must take the consequences. This is another example of *res ipsa loquitur*. But the company works through inspectors, foremen, common workmen, often by contractors, and they in their turn by foremen and workmen. The brick is loose owing to the negligence of one or more of these many subordinates, but which will remain unknown. The negligence of the unknown workman is covered by the breach of the initial duty laid on the company. Thus in this case redress to the injured party is granted, not by reason of any assumption of vicarious liability, but by an appeal to the broad duty laid on the company which excludes any consideration of the actual wrong-doer, whether he be a servant, an independent contractor, or a contractor's servant. The books are full of such cases; the chapters on the laws of Negligence and of Master and Servant teem with them; it is unnecessary for me to elaborate them for you. I have given you sufficient examples of the first principle which deals with the unknown workman. If it can be assumed that he was the servant of another, and was engaged in his master's business when he acted negligently, his master is liable. And again, if it can be shown that there was a duty to do without negligence what the unknown workman has done negligently, or to do what he has failed to do, then he will be liable on whom the duty falls. The unknown workman is ignored. But because he is ignored he is none the less liable for his own misdeed, only he cannot be traced. We know that some one has blundered, but we cannot find the blunderer.

The second principle which affects him tells in his favour, and would protect him even if he were not unknown. It springs from the operation of the law of Remoteness of Damage. Known or unknown, a man's liability for the consequences of a negligent or any other wrongful act ceases at a certain point. When these consequences, causes and consequences, have ceased to follow one another in a natural, probable, or reasonably-to-be-expected manner, the act which set them in motion ceases to be considered in the eye of the law as the cause. That which has unexpectedly intervened and directed the sequence of events into a new channel is the cause, and again the unknown work-man drops out of consideration. The intervening cause may be inanimate, and then the unknown workman goes scot-free; or the intervening cause may be an animate being, whence arises some chance of redress:

for the new act may be itself negligent or otherwise wrongful, and then its author is liable. Curiously enough the law does not discriminate between the two wrongful acts, attributing the effects carefully to their two authors, but in many cases makes the later wrong-doer responsible for all. Take this case. The workmen of a carriage-builder fit the parts of a wheel together negligently. A coachman drives negligently and runs over some one, but the injuries are considerably aggravated by the fact that the badly made wheel breaks down at the critical moment. The coachman, or his master, is liable, although the unknown workman has very materially contributed to the disaster.

It would occupy all the time allotted to me if I were to trace these principles by example through all their ramifications : two more well-known cases will be quite sufficient. There is a portico in front of a railway station ; its roof is being mended ; through a hole in it a plank and a roll of zinc fall on an unsuspecting passenger much to his hurt ; at the moment of the accident he looks up and just catches sight through the aperture of a man's legs. Both parties to the quarrel seem to have taken it for granted that the plank and the zinc fell in consequence of something this man did upon the roof : but the man himself had passed among his fellows and had become the unknown workman, whom neither lawyer nor layman could discover. Once more. A ship is in dry dock having her hull painted ; the dock-owner supplies the staging and all the necessary appliances ; the ropes of the staging give way, and one of the painters is thrown to the bottom of the dock and suffers grievous bodily harm.   It is not difficult to see the unknown workman scamping his work, talking politics perhaps to his mates, instead of seeing that the ropes were sound before they were handed over.   But who he was, by reason of his being one of the great unknown, has become as unimportant as the matter he was discussing. The question of redressing the wrong has to be fought on other grounds : relief has to be given, if at all, as against somebody who did not do the actual wrong. Now, see how fine a distinction separates the case in which relief is given from that in which it is withheld. Arguments of the subtlest kind evolved out of the facts of a ship cast a duty on the dock-owner which he himself had broken.   A duty on the dock-owner, mind you. Intervening contracts removed the question of vicarious liability as between master and servant.   The duty on the person who had supplied the dock-owner with the staging to supply it sound and good according to his contract, and its evident breach, was passed over. The dock-owner had practically invited the person injured to use the dock appliances provided for the work as incident to the use of the dock ; the invitation raised the duty of taking reasonable care that the appliances were in a state fit to be used : and the findings of the jury showed that this duty had been violated.

Arguments no less subtle failed in the railway case either to evolve out of the facts any breach of an analogous duty on the railway company or to attach to it vicarious liability.

Think, then, with regard to the actual cause of all the mischief, how powerless the law is : technical objections innumerable stand in the way of launching writs promiscuously and fishing for causes of action : the barriers between the unknown workman and his unfortunate victim are almost insuperable. The question underlies the whole course of daily existence ; but the law reaches only the fringe of the difficulty, applying to it principles which do not even consider the actual wrong-doer. The unknown workman touches us at every point. How many do you think have assisted in bringing me from my house to this lecture-hall ? How many in making the journey from Tokyo to Yokohama as easy as it is ? How many in constructing the ship that will shortly take me home to England ? Five minutes careless work on the part of any one of them might do incalculable harm to those who have to rely upon their work ; perhaps bring swift destruction upon them. And yet, though the remedy is imperfect, we accept the risks every day without thinking, basing our acceptance on nothing but a reliance on the steadiness of a hundred and more workmen of whom we know absolutely nothing.

There is, however, a compensating element to this incapacity of the law to reach the actual wrong-doer. The British workman, in spite of certain curious crooks in his character, is a most estimable person. Take him all round he is not a careless workman : accidents will

c

happen, of course, but he never yet was known deliberately to scamp his work. If he were going out on
strike at noon, he would be found doing his best work
at half-past eleven. And why? Because he knows,
it has been drilled into him from the earliest days of
his apprenticeship, that human lives may depend on the
excellence of his work: he knows that the public have
confidence in him and feel that they travel with security.
Not one of the ten thousand artificers who have helped
to build a train—the carpenters, the joiners, the iron-
smiths—but knows what depends upon him, and works
with a direct sense of individual responsibility, in spite
of the fact that he knows too that a fault can never
be brought home to him. And we, the public, know
of this sense of responsibility and acquire corresponding
confidence. And thus out of the very powerlessness
of the law have sprung, by action and reaction, that
sense of responsibility and the feeling of confidence
which are absolutely essential to the well-being and
security of the community.

I speak now, through you, to a wider audience.

Can you not see the connection between this branch of
the Law of Negligence and the phrase I originally chose
as the text of my lecture, *shikata ga nai?** English
children are told in their earliest years of a certain man
who was called "Don't care," and who ultimately came
to a bad end—he was hanged, I think. And "Don't
care" had a numerous family about whose fate nursery
history is not so precise, though there can be little doubt

---

* "It cannot be helped;" *lit.*, there is nothing to be done.

that they too suffered the extreme penalty of the law, for their deserts were no greater than their father's. They were christened, " Never mind," " What does it matter? " " Can't be helped," and many other similar names. One of them was born in France ; he had a nasty trick of shrugging his shoulders, and was called " *Tant pis.*" But this expression, *shikata ga nai,* the world has come to take as representative of one queer side of the Japanese character ; and there is not much difference between not caring for consequences after they have happened, and not caring for consequences before they happen. For all observers they stand in the same plane.

The march of Japan from her own civilization to the civilization of the West is marked by the usual incidents : steamboats, railways, omnibuses, telegraphs, electric lights, have appeared one after the other. But something more is necessary. The repose of Western civilization depends on that perfect confidence I have been talking to you about : the perfect confidence of the public in the unknown workmen on whom the safe conduct of these vehicles, the safe transmission of these dangerous elements depend.

This confidence can only be bred of the experience of many years. Does it exist in Japan? It is for you to answer, not for me. If I had to answer, I do not think it would be in the negative. Indeed, I am disposed to say that the wonder which Japan has forced from the nations of the West arises, not from the mere adoption of their appliances, but from the fact that, certainly with regard to all public works, this confidence and this repose have already come into being. Does it extend any deeper? It would be premature as yet to insist upon an answer. It is for the unknown workmen to determine whether by-and-by it shall be yes or no.

But just as the Law of Negligence covers more than mere negligence in the ordinary sense, and includes neglect of proper precaution, recklessness, and heedlessness; so the feeling which *shikata ga nai* expresses may engender all the different forms of disregard of consequences. And just as the duties which the Law of Negligence deals with are precisely identical in point of principle with the duties which, under more definite names, are scattered through the whole law, dealing with every phase of life, and concerning every incident of it; so the spirit of *shikata ga nai* may influence for evil any and every action wherein care is necessary, forethought, right dealing, scrupulous behaviour, honesty of purpose, and consideration for others. And this whether in the narrow spheres of individual life or in the wider scope of public duty.

Young men of Japan, I have something to say to you before I leave your shores. In your hands lies all the future destiny of your country. The generation that is passing away has begun the work: it is but begun, and it is for you to carry it forward to its legitimate end. Are you fit, are you fitting yourselves, for the task that the old men have laid upon your shoulders? Or is your work cramped by that influence for evil of which I have just been talking? Again it is not for me to find the answer; it is for you to be prepared to give it when the nation asks it of you.

There is a cry current among you, Japan for the Japanese : it is for you to show that it is not a mere empty babbling to the air. It springs from the best spirit in the world ; it is one with which an Englishman must always be in sympathy, for in many a page of his own history the cry of England for the English is written larger than life itself. But perverted, it will hurl the shouters into a sea of troubles. It is well for you that you should know that even in the minds of those foreigners who have your country's best interests at heart—believe me they are many—those who see the springs at work beneath the surface, there is a doubt whether the young men of Japan are equal to the stress and strain of the days that lie ahead. They see young men full of high purpose sacrificing themselves and their careers to the cause they have at heart; they see others sacrificing the public good to serve their own ambition! Among your younger officials are many who have realized that a career of usefulness cannot even be begun until they have been as little children in teachableness. But there are others, full of the pride of a newly acquired but somewhat slender stock of learning, who rebel at the presence of foreign advisers in their midst, whose years of study number more than the months of those they have come to guide. There is a magnificent conceit about the possessors of a little knowledge: above all they court public recognition of it; they would be amusing fellows, and an interesting study were they not so dangerous. They at least will never consent to be among the unknown workmen.

But in the work which any State demands, many must be content to remain unknown: and in this State, more than in any, it is necessary that what the unknown workmen do should be done thoroughly, with earnestness of purpose, with a view to the public good, and with a complete effacement of the private aim.

Remember that here, of necessity, young men undertake offices which, in the countries lying to the far east of Japan, are filled by men only after they have reached their riper years of learning and experience. There is no one but wishes success to attend their labours.

As I come to this sheet of my notes I find them much scored and corrected. I had in my mind many harsh and critical things to say: but they are better hinted at than said; for it is ill to leave a country wherein one has been at least half guest with an ungracious word upon the lips. But the other, the adviser half of me, would leave a duty unfulfilled if I did not pray in aid of the good work which so many of your young men are doing a little less self-assertion on the part of some, a little more restraint of that spirit of *shikata ga nai* which must deflect the good from its ultimate aim, the better. What Japan has done in the past, what she is doing to-day, is enough to make her wonder whether it is really nothing to all those who pass by. The nations of the West are very busy with their own affairs, but they are watching, and are ready to admit that it is indeed something to be proud of. But what Japan will do to-morrow concerns her and them more. The time to serve up butter before you on a lordly dish has passed away; it is the time for criticism of the hardest, sternest sort—criticism, not of what the old men have done, but of what the young are doing. Men of the greater sort never yet shrunk from criticism, never yet regretted to admit that they were far the better for it.

Students of the English Law School of Japan, you too will soon have your part to play in public life. When you come, as some of you must come, to administer the laws of your country, I trust you will never shake off the influence of the great Common Law of England whose principles you have been so eager to understand, nor forget to follow in the footsteps of the great Judges who have established them.

LONDON :
PRINTED BY WILLIAM CLOWES AND SONS, LIMITED,
STAMFORD STREET AND CHARING CROSS.

CPSIA information can be obtained
at www.ICGtesting.com
Printed in the USA
380463LV00004B/26